A BOOK OF PRAYERS

A BOOK OF PRAYERS

Erma J. Coburn

iUniverse, Inc.
Bloomington

A BOOK OF PRAYERS

iUniverse books may be ordered through booksellers or by contacting:

iUniverse
1663 Liberty Drive
Bloomington, IN 47403
www.iuniverse.com
1-800-Authors (1-800-288-4677)

ISBN: 978-1-4620-4897-7 (sc)
ISBN: 978-1-4620-4899-1 (hc)
ISBN: 978-1-4620-4898-4 (ebk)

Printed in the United States of America

iUniverse rev. date: 12/16/2011

Photography:
Rohan Preston

Cover Design:
Connecx Multimedia:
www.CONNECXM.com

To

My parents
Mr. and Mrs. Donald and Ethel Hickman
•

My husband and children
Sgt. Albert Vernon Coburn
Myron Vernon and Rhoda Christina Coburn
•

My Brother and Sister
James Hickman and Donella Hickman Hall
•

My Family and Friends

CONTENTS

Acknowledgments

There are so many people to thank for helping to bring this *Book of Prayers* into fruition. First, we want to thank God for giving us the vision and perseverance to complete this Book of Prayers. We would also like to acknowledge the family, friends, prayer partners and supporters, who have consistently prayed with us, for us, and for that we are so grateful.

We offer special appreciation to: Ms. Rhoda Christina Coburn, the author's daughter, who worked diligently contacting and following up with the contributors, to ensure that they would be represented in this exceptional Book. Also, a special thanks to Bishop Patricia Hickman Green who served as a spiritual advisor throughout the entire process, Dr. John A. Reed, Jr., Pastor of Fairview Baptist Church, Vice-President of The National Baptist Convention, and Dr. Patricia Reed, Prayer Coordinator and spiritual supporter of Mrs. Coburn's *Book of Prayers*.

We are indebted to Dr. John L. Smith, Jr., Former President of Fisk University for his encouragement, support, and guidance to ensure the Book was completed.

We are also, very grateful and appreciative to Dr. JoAnn Clark, retired English Professor from Langston University, who gave tirelessly of her time and commitment to editing the manuscript which accelerated the pace for publication.

The contributors are an extraordinary group of world-wide ministers. Other contributors include family, church members, educators, administrators, and special neighbors. It was due to their love for the author that all of the contributors were honored and enthusiastically agreed to submit a prayer for inclusion. And we are thankful for the time and effort each one put forth.

Furthermore, we would like to specifically acknowledge The Coburn, Hickman, Shannon, and Smith Families and the author's siblings; Donald Hickman, Jr., Rudolph, Juel, Olivia, Patricia, and Lawrence Hickman, who have been so supportive of the family's *Prayer Warrior* throughout the years.

Contributors

Elder Kenny Blackwell
Pastor Henry T. Busby, Sr.
Ms. Delores June Cobb
Ms. Rhoda Christina Coburn
Reverend James Flagg
Reverend Scott Gordon
Pastor Loren Green
Bishop Patricia Hickman Green
Reverend William Holloway
Reverend Oscar Howard
Pastor Clarence D. Maynor, Jr.
Dr. George Calvin McCutchen, Sr.
Dr. Mozella G. Mitchell
Mrs. Doris Mullen
Mrs. Angela Shannon Preston
Dr. John A. Reed, Jr.
Mrs. Clara Richards
Dr. Francina Thomas
Mrs. Edna Marz and Nettie Tisdale
Reverend Robert E. Warren

Introduction

Ask, and it shall be given you; seek, and ye shall find; knock, and it
shall be opened unto you: For everyone that asketh receiveth; and
he that seeketh findeth; and to him that
knocketh it shall be opened.

St. Matthew 7:7-8.

There is a divine power in prayer. In prayer, there is peace,
hope and healing. Many books have been written about
Prayer. In this collection, you will find a rich variety that
will sustain and comfort you in your every day life. They are
written by Evangelist Erma Coburn, with contributions by
esteemed ministers and special friends.

These prayers, including various forms, have been taught
and prayed within our family from generation to generation.
Additionally, The author has prayed with and for families
throughout the world, including several countries in Africa,
in Israel (The Holy Land), the Caribbean, Austria, and Spain.
These prayers have been spoken to God in good times and
difficult times, always with the understanding that God is
listening and will respond.

Many years ago, the author spent time teaching her siblings
the importance of prayer, and we have greatly benefited.
Prayer has always been the center of her life and ours.
Evangelist Coburn loves to Pray; she continually talks with
God and the Lord truly hears her prayers!!! She taught us that
Prayer is the lifeline to our Lord and Savior Jesus Christ. And
because of her love for people, especially members of God's
Church, we felt she would be extremely pleased that her
Pastor, Dr. John A. Reed, Jr. and some of her other ministerial
colleagues, family, church members and friends were invited
to contribute prayers to her Book of Prayers. It is this special
group of "Prayer Warriors" that has made this collection of
prayers very rich, different, and special.

These prayers, written over a period of more than 15 years, took place during Coburn's annual visits to Florida. However, because of her increasingly busy schedule involving mothering two children, developing, teaching, and presenting at workshops, preaching and praying, the writing of prayers all but ceased. More serious time and effort were dedicated to her missionary work which included caring for the sick and needy, visiting hospitals, correction facilities and nursing homes in local, national and international communities. At that time, she felt that mission work was more important than the completion of this book.

Therefore, because of our untiring love and our appreciation for all of the prayers that were prayed for and with us, we decided to complete this collection of prayers as a special gift to her and for all humanity to enjoy and be spiritually enriched.

The Bible shows us the power of prayer. Through numerous scriptures, we see God respond miraculously when people pray. Using God's word as a light, in this unique Book of Prayers, each petition is supported by a related verse to further illuminate the prayer's meaning.

The Lord has made this book possible because the need for prayer in this world is so great. This Book of inspirational prayers will satisfy many human needs. This Book of Prayers has been a work of love It is our hope that it will soothe the soul and calm the spirit, and thereby make a thoughtful gift for anyone who needs encouragement through prayer.

We hope your journey throughout the following pages will bless you and help you to become a blessing to others.

Juel Hickman Shannon Smith, Ph.D.
Tampa, Florida

1
Opening
Prayer

*And all things, whatsoever ye shall ask
in prayer, believing, ye shall receive.
Matthew 21:22.*

What is Prayer?

Prayer is one of the greatest tools
one can have in the world because it opens
the door to a dialogue with God.
You are establishing that connection within your heart
and mind and giving yourself the
opportunity to have a
deeper experience with God.
A prayer can be as simple as "Thank you God,"
or it can be an unending dialogue about
anything you want to share with God.
Prayer is welcoming God into your life and your needs.

O Mighty and Heavenly Father
We thank You that we can communicate with You.
That You are my intimate Friend.
I want prayer to become more and more
a part of my life so that each and everything
I do will be a prayer
that ties me closer
to You.

Amen.

God of All Creations

Trust in the Lord with all thine heart; and lean not unto
thine own understanding. In all thy ways acknowledge Him,
and He shall direct thy paths. Proverbs 3:5-6

Almighty God, the author and
preserver of all creation. We
come today feeling our
insufficiencies, but we come.
We have come from the market
place of life through the arena
to the alter. And here we are;
we need strength, motivation,
and consolation for the task that
You and You alone can give.

We realize we have sinned
and come short of Thy word,
but we ask that You would look
beyond our faults, please
Sir Jesus, and supply our needs.
Lord, we want to be better people,
live better, act better, and love more.

And when we, too, must go the way of all mankind, We don't want to be like slaves going to our dungeon, but, we want to look over a well-spent life as we enter that land where everyday is Sunday and the Sabbath has no end.

Thank You Lord,
and
much obliged!

Amen.

The Power of the Lord

What? know ye not that your body is the temple of the Holy Ghost
which is in you, which ye have of God, and ye are not your own?
For ye are bought with a price: therefore, glorify God in your body,
and in your spirit, which are God's. Corinthians 6:19-20

O God our Father,
We come to Thee in the humblest manner we know
how, thanking You for life, and the blessings of
life. We realize in everything we do, we need the
presence of Your power.

Lord, we know our own inadequacies
and shortcomings. And we know that
we have no power of our own.
We know that we are weak and feeble, and
We know that we are finite creatures who are here
but a moment.

We recognize that all power is in Your hands.
So, Lord, teach us to pray with faith so that our
lives will demonstrate Your presence,
Your powers, and Your gifts.

Amen.

A Prayer of Thanks

Give thanks unto the Lord, call upon His name,
make known His deeds among the people. Sing unto Him,
sing Psalms unto Him, talk ye of all His wondrous works.
1 Chronicles 16:8-9

Almighty God, we thank You for another day
As we enter into Your presence.
Lord, and we ask You to please lead and guide us
from one degree of grace to another.
Sometimes, we wonder if it had not been for
the Lord on our side, where would we be.

Lord, we thank You for food on the table,
clothes on our backs, shelter over our heads,
a bed to sleep in, and a stove to keep us warm.
Lord, we thank You for friends and family, and a
mind to pick and choose our own praying ground.
Lord, we thank You for the peace
that only You can give that peace
that surpasses all understanding,
through Christ our Lord.

Amen.

Hallelujah!

Life is A Great Privilege

Trust in the Lord, and do good; so shalt thou dwell in the land,
and verily thou shalt be fed. Delight thyself also in the Lord;
and He shall give thee the desires of thine heart
Psalm 37:3-4

Almighty God, teach us to number our days
that we may apply our hearts to wisdom.
Thou hast made our days fruitful of suggestion from heaven,
so that we need not stumble, if we will but look at Thy
providence, and listen to Thy law, and make Thy word a
lamp unto our feet, and a light to our pathway.

For we are living in a dark world,
and without You and Your grace, we
just stumble through life, as if we have
no meaning. We realize there are so many
opportunities in Thy word that we could
enjoy, if we seek the Lord while He may be
found, and call upon Him while He is near.
Lord, we thank You for the gift of life and a sound
mind, too, even through it has in it pain and sorrows, its
disappointments, yet, notwithstanding, it is a daily struggle
with death, and in its most beauteous forms, it runs along
the valley which is full of graves. Yet, is life a great privilege,
a keen joy,a splendid call to upward behavior and noble
conduct; a challenge to the self to become
enlarged, ennobled, and glorified?
When we are stung by its pains and blighted
by it disappointments, may we lean totally
upon divine guidance and strength
that has kept us through the years.

Lord please, help us in our faults and failures,
to become better men and women. Pardon our
sins, for they are great; Wash us in the holy
sacrificial blood, that blood that reaches to the
highest mountain, and flows to the lowest
valley, that blood that was shed for the
remission of our sins. That
blood that will never, never, never,
lose its power. It has stood through
generation after generation.
And it has never lost a drop of its power.

Hallelujah

See how great a love
the Father has bestowed upon us,
that we should be called children of God;
and such we are.

For this reason, the world does not know us,
because it did not know Him.

Beloved, now we are children of God,
and it has not appeared as yet
what we shall be.
We know that when He appears,
we shall be like Him
because we shall see Him just as He is.

And everyone who has this hope fixed on Him
purifies himself, just as He is pure.

1 John 3:1-3 NASB

God As A Door Opener

Ask and it will be given to you; seek and you will find;
knock and the door will be opened to you.
For everyone who asks receives;
he who seeks finds; and to him who knocks,
the door will be opened.
Matthew 7:7

Father God we come this morning
With bowed heads and outreaching hearts
Thanking You for all of Your many blessings;
We come realizing that You have been better to
us than we know how to be to ourselves.

We know that You are a way maker;
For You have made a way out of no way;
A door opener where many doors have been
shut to educational opportunities.
You are a problem solver for the many
issues we are faced with today.
Lord Jesus, we know what You have done and what
You can do. You are a light to our path and a lamp
to our feet. We know You as a bridge over troubled
waters, a mender of broken hearts and hung
down heads. Lord, we realize You have brought
us a very long way, and
We realize we have a long way to go.
In Jesus name we pray.

Amen.

God As King

And He hath on His vesture and on His thigh a name
written King of Kings and Lord of Lords. Revelations 19:16

Lord, our Lord,
how excellent is Thou name
in all the earth. For Thou has made us
lower than the angels and crowned us
with wisdom and knowledge from
on high. We know that You are
our King and soon will be coming
to restore us unto Yourself.

Jesus is looking for us to have a life
of prayer and repentance. God give us
the deep appreciation for humanity and
mankind, and order our steps in Your way
and in Your word. We love and appreciate
You for all the wonderful things
You have given us.
Lord, we want to always
be Your servant.

Amen.

Because He Lives

Jesus said to her, "I am the resurrection,
and the life. He that believeth in Me,
though he were dead, yet shall he live. And
Whoever liveth and believeth in Me shall never
die. Believeth thou this?"

John 11:25-26

Because He lives . . . I can face tomorrow
Because He lives . . . All fear is gone,
Because I know, He holds my future and
Life is worth the living, just because He lives.

O mighty and heavenly Father,
We come as humble as we know how, to say
Thank You. Thank You for the many blessings
You have bestowed upon us.

Thank You for waking us up this morning,
clothed in our right mind.
Thank You for the food, clothing and
shelter, for we take these
things for granted so many times.

We realize sorrow is but a night,
but joy comes in the morning. And Lord,
we need that joy; we need that peace
that surpasses all understanding.
Lord please, bless all families
Bless the sick and shut-in,
Bless the Home and Homeless,
Bless the Aids and HIV-infected victims,
Bless the drug dependents and alcoholics.

13

Help them to know
that You are God and You are still in
the business of healing. You are indeed
a miracle-worker, and You have
never, never lost a case!

Lord, please help there to be world peace,
Bless the church; the church leaders throughout
this country. Help us to know . . . and be mindful
of the fact that life is worth the living because
You live!

Amen.

A Prayer for Strength

The Lord is my strength and my shield; my heart trusted in Him,
and I am helped: therefore my heart greatly rejoiceth;
and with my song will I praise Him. Psalm 28:7

———————

Father in Jesus' name,
We pray for every joined hand
Every feeble knee, every broken heart,
Every runaway child,
Those that are in correction homes and
Halfway houses, those that are in search
for self. And help them to understand that
when they find God they find self.

Lord, we pray for those who have come up
the rough side of the mountain with little or no hope.
But in our climb between here and there,
You sent us faith to realize
that we could not make it on our own.
It was You all the time.

Lord, as we pray for those to the right and
left of us, we ask You to lighten life's load,
And help us to realize that we can do
All things through Christ who strengthens us.

Amen.

15

II
Prayers:
Relationship With God

God, thank You for all the ways
You reveal Yourself to us.

Seeking God

Before I formed you in the womb I knew you, before you were born
I set you apart; I appointed you as a prophet to the nations.
Jeremiah 1:5, NIV translation

O Great and Holy One,
My Anchor and My Rock, My Balm of Gilead,
My Mighty Counselor, Holy, Holy, Holy, is Your name.

You called my mother and father,
their mother and father,
the generations before, then called me
through Your string of ancestors.

I am because You are. Before life taught me
problems and pain, joy and gladness,
You had a vision and a purpose for me.

There is no human struggle too big or too tiny
that You cannot meet with victory.

Whether, it is an aching body
or a wounded heart, You are Jehovah,
the Great Healer, the Ointment poured forth,
My Jesus and My All.
Victory is in Your name, Peace is in Your name,
Love is Your name.
Let us remember in our midnight hours
that You are Omnipresent,
Let us remember to whisper Savior, to reach for
Your garment,
or feel for Your hand, and to seek Your face.

Amen.

— Angela Shannon

ERMA J. COBURN

A Thirst For God

And did all drink the same spiritual drink:
for they drank of that spiritual Rock that followed them:
and that Rock was Christ. 1 Corinthians 10:4

───────────

Almighty God, our soul thirst for Thee
Thou Art the living water and the river of God
is full of water. We know that You alone can
quench the thirst of the soul.

We hear the voice of Jesus Christ, Thy Son, saying
"If any man thirst let him come unto Me and drink".
We hear the voice of the prophet crying.
"So everyone that thirst, come ye to the waters".
The spirit of God is saying, come.
Let him that is thirsty come
and drink freely of
The Water of Life.

Lord, You said "come," and the blind, lame,
and many who were very sick came to be healed.
So we want to thank You, Lord, and praise
Your Holy name, for providing a river that runs
from the throne of God
And if we drink of this water, we will never
thirst again. Lord, please give us
this living water

Amen.

Surrendering To God

Offer the sacrifices, of righteousness,
and put your trust in the Lord. Psalm 4:5

I surrender all to Jesus, all to Him I freely give
all to Thee my blessed Savior, I Surrender all.

O God our Father
We honor Your name
We surrender to Your Will and
enter into a deeper relationship with You.
Lord, we surrender all to You.
Please bless us to be humble in Your sight
And teach us to walk in the way that You
would have us to go.
We surrender all to You; please take our
broken spirits, depressed spirits
Contrite spirits and mold them to Your glory.
Lord, please take our mind, body, soul,
spirit and our entire life into Your hands,
so that we may continue to serve You
all the days of our lives.
Forever and ever.

Amen.

Thank You for Life

For God so loved the world, that He gave His only begotten
Son that whosoever believeth in Him should not perish,
but have everlasting life. John 3:16

———————

Our Father in Heaven,
Again we come to Thy
presence to greet You
In the Holy Spirit.
Father, we say as Your
children, we are grateful.

We thank You for life as it is
right now. I pray for the world
itself, as it is so slandered right
now. "We have sinned against
God" and Father, as Your children,
we must repent.

We thank You that we are able
to send this prayer.
We thank You for our loved ones.
We thank You for our lives.
It is in Your name we pray.

Amen.

—Reverend Robert E. Warren (Uncle Bob)
West Bethel Missionary Baptist Church
McAlester, Oklahoma

How Great Thou Art

Great is the Lord, and greatly to be praised;
and His greatness is unsearchable. Psalm 145:3

———————

Oh Lord, my God when I in awesome wonder,
and consider all that Thy hands have made,
How great Thou art, how great Thou Art.

Sometimes life demands one to look into his
inner self, and search the walls of thy soul,
and as I look into the interior of this marvelous
body that Thy alone has made, my soul looks
back and wonder, how great Thou art.

Lord, You walked with Your hands stretched to the heavens
and out into space, and stood on nothing because there was
nothing to stand on.
How Great Thou Art.

Lord, You spoke into space,
And the world began to materialize. Lord,
this helps us to remember how great Thou art.

When we consider how You made the moon,
stars, planets and the vast universe how great
Thou art! We thank You for being our God.

Amen.

A Prayer To The Lord

If we confess our sins,
He is faithful and just to forgive us our sins,
and to cleanse us from all unrighteousness. 1 John 1:9

———————

Lord, we confess that we have sinned
by tolerating evils and impurities
that are not appropriate for Your holy people.
We ask You to, please Lord, forgive us
and cleanse us, set us free from any desire to
hold on to impurities; change our hearts so
that we will be obedient to You.
Lord, help us to be as saved
as a saved sinner can be.

Thank You for the purity
and Godly character You are
bringing into our lives.

Amen.

Pastor Clarence Darold Maynor
Triangle Pointe Fellowship Church
Durham, North Carolina

Lord Give Us
An Humble Spirit

Pride goeth before destruction and an haughty spirit before
a fall. Better it is to be of an humble spirit with the lowly, than
to divide the spoil with the proud. Proverbs 16:18-19

Spirit of the Living God,
fall fresh on me,
break me, melt me, mold me, fill me.
Spirit of the living God, fall fresh on me.
Almighty and most merciful God, as
we make our way through the many days
of trials and tribulations that are ahead,
please give us a spirit of humility
That is pleasing to You.

For all that we have done, and all
of the knowledge that we have acquired,
help us to understand that it is not by our hands,
but they are the blessing that You have provided
for us. Lord, please keep us with a humble
spirit, so we may continue to do Your will.

Amen.

Reverend James Flagg
Atlanta, Georgia

How Excellent Is Thy Name

O Lord our Lord, how excellent is Thy name
in all the earth. Psalm 8:9

O Lord, how excellent is Thy name in all the earth.
For we know You as a searcher of our hearts,
and we tremble before Thee.
The light of Thine eyes fall upon the innermost parts
of the heart, and there is nothing hidden from Thee.

The darkness and the light are both alike unto Thee.
Lord, we visualize You as the wings of the morning
that carry us away into the wild blue yonder.
You somehow hide us in the cliff of the rock.
We realize there is nothing that You do not know.
You know the known and unknown places in our heart.
We realize we are like sheep that have gone astray,
We have each turned away from You.

But Father, forgive us of all of our secret sins,
There are so many. Father, You said; "Though your
Sin be as scarlet, You can and will wash us,
and we will become as white as snow."
Lord, please restore the joy of our salvation.
How excellent is Thy name in all the earth.

Amen.

A Prayer for Repentance

Thou has neither part nor lot in this matter: for thy heart is not right in the sight of God. Repent therefore of this thy wickedness, and pray God, if perhaps the thought of thine heart may be forgiven thee. For I perceive that thou art in gall of bitterness, and in the bond of iniquity. Acts 8:21-23

———

Help me Lord,
to be discerning and not let others
lead me astray with their falsehood.
May the fruit of my life be an example
of a follower of Christ,
Amen.

———

Oh, to be like Thee, Blessed Redeemer.
This is my constant longing and prayer.
Gladly, I will forfeit all of the earth's
treasures for Jesus, Thy perfect
likeness to wear.

Of whom we have many things to say,
and hard to be uttered, seeing ye are
dull of hearing. Hebrew 5:11; And
this will we do, if God permit. Hebrew 6:3

Amen.

Mrs. Doris Mullen
Prayer Warrior Sapulpa, Oklahoma

A Prayer for Reconciliation

And all things are of God, who hath reconciled us
to Himself by Jesus Christ, and hath given to us
the ministry of reconciliation. 2 Corinthians 5:18

O, Gracious God
ruling the earth and its people not by terror
but in love, we worship You.
We confess that too often our words hurt others
And our deeds are selfish. Forgive us.
In this time of uncertainty and fear,
help us to love our enemies and do good
to those who hate us.

As Your servants, You requested us to spread love, joy, and
reconciliation where people are divided—Mother against
daughter, Father against son. You opened this way for us
so that Your church may help the poor and all of humanity.
Lord help us to fulfill Your request.

Amen.

III
Prayers For Families

Bless all families, God. Give them strength
love and patience. Use them to Your glory. Amen.

Prayer for Families

And it shall come to pass afterward, that I will pour
out My spirit upon all flesh; and your sons and your daughters
shall prophesy, your old men shall dream dreams, your young
men shall see visions. Joel 2: 28

O Lord God, we thank You for our families.
You have given us many wonderful children
And You have blessed them in and for Your
service. They have not always done as they
should, but we thank You Lord.
We thank You for being a God of second chances.
Through good times and bad times
You have always been there.
Thank You, Lord, for loving us enough to give us
healthy bodies, minds, spirits, and a great heart.

Thank You, Lord, for our families, and our extended
families . . . You have been better to us than we have
been to ourselves. Thank You Lord for teaching us
Your will and Your way. Thank You for shelter, food,
and books to read. We thank You Lord for Your
Holy Bible. No wonder, David said
"Thy word have I hid in my heart, that
I might not sin against Thee."

Thank You, Lord
Thank You, Lord
Thank You, Lord

Amen.

God Will Supply Our Needs

But my God shall supply all your need according to His
riches in glory by Jesus Christ. Philippians 4:19

O God, our God how excellent
is Thy Name in all the Earth.
Father, we come to the Throne of Grace
just to say; "thank You."

Thank You for all You have done, all
You are doing, and all that You are going to do.
Lord, we are living in troublesome times,
so we are requesting prayer
for the suffering of all mankind,
the need of the homeless,
the cry of the prisoners,
the pains of the sick and the injured,
the sorrow of the bereaved,
the helplessness of the aged and the weak.

Lord, we ask that You strengthen,
Protect and relieve them of their pain,
and bless them according
to their various needs. These are the
blessings we ask in Jesus' name.

Amen.

Pastors Loren and Patricia Green
New Life Family Outreach Church
Tulsa, Oklahoma

Family Blessings

That in blessing I will bless thee, and in multiplying I will multiply
Thy seed as the stars of the heaven, and as the sand which is upon the
seashore; and thy seed shall possess the gate of his enemies.
Genesis 22:17

O God, our heavenly Father,
We ask You to bless all families.

We entrust to You, the members
of our families, both near and far.
We ask that You supply their
needs, guide their footsteps, and
keep them safe in body and soul.

Lord, we ask for Peace, Peace, in
our homes and within our families.
Bless us to continue to grow in love
for each other.

Lord these are the blessings we
humbly ask in Your Name and we will
continue to give You all the praise.

Amen.

Remembering Mothers' Prayers

Thus saith the Lord the Maker thereof, the Lord that
formed it, to establish it; the Lord is His name; Call upon
Me, and I will answer thee, and shew thee great and mighty
things, which thou knowest not. — Jeremiah 33: 2-3

Lord our Father,
In yesteryears it seems that families
had a special love that was passed
from generation to generation.
Mothers had a special love and knew
when to stroke or love each child.
There were never too many
children to love.

As we reminisce
over the years,
Mothers are so precious.
They planted us in the right path
And prayed daily that the children
would be what the Lord wanted
them to be.
Mothers would always pray before
The children went to school and at night
Before the children went to bed.
The children felt safe and if anything
would happen, God would take care
of them.

And in our prayers of yesterday.
our Mothers would always say,
"If it is the Lord's will,
we will see you tomorrow."
The Lord was the center of our lives.
So, it is no wonder we must pray daily
because prayer is a habit.
Lord, thank You for today and
all of our yesterdays.

Amen.

A Mother of All Seasons

I was glad when they said unto me,
Let us go into the house of the Lord. Psalm 122:1

———————

Thank God for Mothers;
Mothers are a blessing
throughout our lives
and during all seasons.

They are there to give us guidance,
advice and hope no matter what the
problem may be.
We thank You God for blessing us
with Mothers. They are someone who
always has a positive word;
to bless and to lift up a bowed down head.
May God continue to bless Mothers
throughout the world.
Love and Blessings!

Amen.

Reverend Oscar Howard
Macedonia Baptist Church
Sapulpa, Oklahoma

A Woman of God
A Role Model for Christians

Blessed is the man that walketh not in the counsel of the ungodly, nor standeth in the way of sinners, nor sitteth in the seat of the scornful. But his delight is in the law of the LORD; and in His law doth He meditate day and night. And He shall be like a tree planted by the rivers of water, that bringeth forth His fruit in His season; His leaf also shall not wither; and whatsoever He doeth shall prosper. Psalm 1: 1-3

My Lord and my God,
Thank you for the dear ones whose lives
are examples, a book that is seen rather than read.
Thank You that Your love is still manifested in people here
on earth: a smile, a kind word, a reminder that Your love
will never fail.

Thank You Lord, for showing us that our
Christian walk means more than our Christian talk.
Let my light shine through, that those who are blind might
get a glimpse of You.

Thank You Lord, for teaching us to forgive,
For You said, "Do unto others as you would have
them do unto you." Lord you are the example,
You asked for their forgiveness and said,
" . . . for they know not what they do."
I beseech You, father, on behalf of all those
who have not learned to trust You,
and thank You for all the things
You brought me through.

37

Now, Lord, I ask Your special blessing on
those who follow You, and pray that others
will find their way, too.

As the cold of snow in time of harvest, so is a
faithful messenger to them that send Him:

For He refresheth the soul of His masters.
Thank You Dear Lord for faithful messengers
and especially the ones You put in our lives
to guide us our whole life through.

Amen.

Rhoda Christina Coburn
Oklahoma City, Oklahoma

God's Special People

I have showed you all things, how that so labouring ye
ought to support the weak, and to remember the words of the
Lord Jesus how He said, "it is more blesseth to give
than to receive." Acts 20:35

O Almighty and merciful God,
With life as complicated as it is,
and it seems that people don't want
to be bothered with anyone any more.

Then, there is a knock on the door and
there comes that very special person, that
God has sent with pie or cake, flowers or
dinner in hand with a prayer so special you
know it's heaven's blessing.

Who could it be with such a big smile
seasoned with a little salt and always with grace.
Of course, our Spiritual Warrior.

Who is always working in the field trying to
please Jesus, any way possible from throughout
America to Africa. This servant does nothing
for fortune and certainly not for fame. But all in
Jesus' name. Blessings!

Amen.

Mother Clara Richards
Oklahoma City, Oklahoma

39

O Lord, Thou hast searched me, and known me.
Thou knowest my down sitting and mine uprising,
Thou understandest my thought afar off.
Thou compasses my path and my
lying down, and art acquainted with all my ways.
For there is not a word in my tongue, but, lo, O Lord,
Thou knowest it altogether. Thou hast beset me
behind and before, and laid thine hand upon me.
Such knowledge is too wonderful for me; it is high,
I cannot attain unto it. Whither shall I go from thy spirit?
Or whither shall I flee from Thy presence?
If I ascend up into heaven, Thou are there:
if I make my bed in hell, behold, Thou art there.
If I take the wings of the morning,
and dwell in the uttermost parts of the sea;
Even there shall Thy hand lead me, and
Thy right hand shall hold me.
Psalm 139:1-10

Amen.

Lord: You Know Who We Are

And now, brethren, I commend you to God, and to
the word of His grace, which is able to build you up, and give you
an inheritance among all them which are sanctified. Acts 20: 32

———————

O Lord our God! You know who we are;
people with good consciences and with bad,
persons who are content and those who are
discontent, the certain and the uncertain,
Christians of conviction and Christians by
convictions, those who believe, those who half
believe, those who disbelieve.

And You know where we have come from;
from the circle of relatives,
acquaintances and friends or from
the greatest loneliness;
from a life of quiet prosperity
or from manifold confusion and distress;
from family relationships that are
well ordered or from those disordered or
under stress; from the inner circle of
the Christian community or
from its outer edges.

But now, we all stand before You,
in all our differences, yet alike in that
we would all be lost without You.
We would be lost without Your grace,
For it is Your Grace that is promised and
made available to all of us in Your
Son Jesus Christ.

We are here together to praise You,
to magnify You and to thank You for
the many blessings that You have given
to us throughout the years.

Lord, we ask You to please continue to
fill our hearts with Thy truth and Thy
light, and we will continue to give
You all the praise.
In Jesus' Name.

Amen.

Mrs. Barth
Los Angeles, California

IV
Educational Prayers

*Lord, bless us to keep growing educationally,
spiritually closer and closer to You.*

A Prayer for Educators

I will instruct thee and teach thee in the way which
thou shall go: I will guide thee with Mine eye. Psalm 32:8

Father, God, we thank You for school days.
During the early years, education was
So important. It appeared as if we were
taking an empty bucket and letting it down
deep into a well of fresh water. It was as if
we were saying, "Lord fill their minds and let
it overflow into Your world of knowledge."

Don't let the children leave until they have
mastered the reading, writing, science,
arithmetic, and all of the subject matters
that are required to make them a better
student. Lord, we thank You for teachers;
teachers with a love for students, and the
subject matter, teachers who would not
let students remain in their classrooms
without challenging their minds.
In those days, students were eager
to get to class so that they wouldn't
miss any of the instructions.

They were greeted with love, and were
taught with love, and they understood
with love. And if there was a problem,
the teacher took care of it immediately,
and later parents were informed of any
misbehavior that occurred that day. And
when students arrived at home, their
parents took the "board of education",
and reminded them of the purpose for
being in school. Lord, we thank You,
for helping to solve the problems of
educating our children. During those
school days, the village worked . . .
because it takes a village to raise
a child.

Amen.

Good Morning Lord
A Teacher's Prayer

And He took them up in His arms, put His
hands upon them, and blessed them. Mark 10:16

───────────

O Lord, God of life,
as we walk into our classrooms daily,
please, give each child that hunger
and thirst for knowledge
that is needed today to keep them
on the right path of learning.

Lord, help us to continue to be committed
to teaching and educating the children,
for they are in our educational institutions
to learn. You handmade these children, and
they are as fresh as the morning dew, and
they are hungry for today's food
from the Fountain of Knowledge.
Lord please, feed them with
knowledge and understanding.

Amen.

A Prayer For Children

Train up a child in the way he should go and when he is old,
he will not depart from it" Proverb 22:6.

O Lord, as we teach the children whom
You have entrusted to our care,
Help us to instill in them the courage
to stand up for what is right,
Even when no one else will.
Help them to realize that courageous
People lose some of the battles of life,
But they will win the greater victory.

Lord, as we teach the children
You have given to us, help us to be the teacher
You are calling on in these evil days. Help us to live
so that our children will see You in our lives.
We don't want to only talk, but to live as Your servant
in times like these. Lord, teach us to live like You,
love like You, talk like You, walk like You,
and be patient to those that are less fortunate
than we are. Lord, teach us Your will and Your way,
so that others may see You in our lives.

Amen.

A Prayer For Health

Fear thou not, for I am with thee; be not dismayed; for I am thy God;
I will strengthen thee; yea, I will help thee; yea
I will uphold thee with the right hand of My
righteousness. — Isaiah 41:10

O Lord God, maker of heaven and earth.
We come to ask You for Your infinite
mercy, a gift of health, comfort and
prosperity. We realize our strength is made
perfect in weakness, so that we may know
You in a very special way.

Lord help us to be content in whatever
state of health we are in, for we realize
in this life, there are good days and bad.

Lord, please continue to strengthen us
to go back to our duties and to bear
with patience our sickness and suffering.
Lord help us to realize that all things
work together for the good of those
who love the Lord.

Amen.

49

ERMA J. COBURN

A Prayer For
HealthCare Professionals

Yea, He loved the people; all His saints are in Thy hand: and they
sat down at Thy feet; every one shall receive
of Thy words. Deuteronomy 33:3

———————

Almighty and everlasting God,
from whom all blessings flow.
We pray for all of our health
professionals.

Those with the gentle
touch of the hand of God.
Lord, we are thankful that
You are present in all of our
healthcare professionals.
Lord, let them know
that You are with them.

Continue to bless those
You have anointed
to work on the human body
that You created.

Lord, please give them the
strength and courage to continue
to nurture each patient as
if they were their very own child.
Lord, You are so wonderful
to create each individual with a
special gift of love and to
reach out to those that are
less fortunate than they.

We are thankful that You have
helped us in our suffering, and
restored our strength. We will
forever show gratitude for a
constant and faithful service
rendered from our doctors.

Amen.

Erma J. Coburn

Teach Us to Understand

All scripture is given by inspiration of God, and is profitable for doctrine,
for reproof, for correction, for instruction in righteousness: That the man
of God may be perfect, thoroughly furnished unto
all good works. 2 Timothy 3:16-17

Almighty God,
teach us the value of things,
for we know them not.
Give us the spirit of
Understanding so that we
may be wise men and women.

Lord, open our minds so that
we may understand the scriptures;
open our eyes that we may behold
wondrous things out of Thy law;
open our hearts so that we may
become more and more like You.

Christ of Glory,
Save us from ourselves
may we live in God
and in God we must put our trust.

Lord please, increase our strength;
when we are blind with tears,
may the eyes of our soul be wide open;
when the cloud fills the heaven,
may we hear a voice in the cloud,
always the same sweet voice,
calling us to Thy Son,
The Son, Thy Son.
In Him may we find the cradle,
the cross, the crown.
All in All

Amen.

V
God's Guidance

O God, guide us toward a wider reading of Thy
Word, that Thy word may be a lamp unto our
feet and a light unto our path. These are the
blessings we ask in your name.
Amen.

God's Guidance

0 house of Jacob, come ye, and let us
walk in the light of the Lord. Isaiah 2:5.

If when you give, the very best of your
service — telling the world, that the Savior has
come — Be not dismayed when men don't believe
you for He will understand and say, "well done."
Lord, there is a bend in the road of our lives;
we need Your instant guidance and direction
to do as You would have us to do. We realize
that without You, there is no life at all.
So Lord, teach us to number our days and
apply our hearts to wisdom.

O Lord, as we go into the evening of life,
we ask that You would take us by the hand
and lead us from one degree of grace to
another. Lord, please help us to pick up the
emptiness in our lives and look to You for
complete richness of Thy word. Teach us to
acknowledge You in all our ways.

Amen.

Guide Me O, Great Jehovah

Behold, God is my salvation; I will trust, and not be afraid:
for the Lord JEHOVAH is my strength and my song; He also is
become my salvation. Isaiah 12: 2

Our Father the light of the world,
the great Jehovah, the creator of
this universe. We come with bowed
heads and humbled hearts thanking
You for watching over each of us
last night, and awakening each of us
this morning to a new day. We want
to pause and say "thank You Lord,"
for supplying our needs in order that
we may have sustained life, health,
and strength.

Master, You have allowed these
Blessings to fall upon us not because
we have been obedient to Your will but because
of Your mercy and Your love; You looked
beyond our faults and saw our need.
Thank You, Lord.

You are such a good and understanding Father
always willing to forgive: we pray right now,
that You will forgive us for our wrong doings.
Create in each one of us a clean heart and a renewed spirit to
walk humbly in the path of righteousness. Clean our hearts
to obey Thou word, we recognize and we realize that we are
living in evil times and what we are experiencing was told
many, many years ago. But we are so grateful that You sent
the Holy Spirit to be our comforter.

In times such as these, we want to pause
and say "thank You Lord." Bless all the leaders of the world
and help them to realize that You and only You, have the
answers to all of our problems.
Help us to recognize that You are the best
counselor we will ever experience. Bless those
who are sick and shut-in; heal their bodies,
and increase their strength, we pray. Let each
of us strive to be Christ-like with a mission that was given
by You, to go into all parts of the world and spread Jesus
died for all sins, and that we can all be heirs
of His Kingdom, if we only believe.

We thank You for that assurance
that You have given us in Your word.
Master, we pray that each of us will be
stronger ambassadors for Your word.
We will sing, without a doubt,
and with sincere hearts;
with a firm acclamation on Christ
the solid rock I stand, all other grounds
are sinking sand. This is our prayer;
we petition these requests in
Jesus' name, Your son who died on
the cross that we my have
everlasting life.

Amen.

The Lord Is My Light

In Him was life; and the life was the light of men.
John 1:4. This then is the message which we have
heard of Him, and declare unto you, that God is light,
and in Him is no darkness at all. I John 1:5

O, God,
Help us to always know and
understand that You are the light
of the world. Thou has designed us,
for great living and we would
not disappoint Thee.

Thou hast given us,
bodies to be the temple of Thy
Holy Spirit and we would keep
them clean and fit.

Thou hast endowed us with
minds to think, to dream, to love;
and we would consecrate them
to high callings. These are the
blessings we ask in Your name.

Amen.

A Prayer: Not to Stray

But they that wait upon the Lord shall renew their strength;
they shall mount up with wings as eagles; they shall run, and
not be weary; and they shall walk, and not faint. Isaiah 40: 31

If when you give the best of your service,
telling the world, that the Savior has come,
be not dismayed when men don't believe you.
He will understand and say well done.

O Lord, we open our souls, and ask You to wash us
through and through so that we will not
stray away from the fold.

Lord, as we stand on the brink of humanity,
staring eternity in the face. We pray for Your
guidance to continue in the path of righteousness
for Your name's sake. Lord, please don't let us stray away
from Thou bleeding side.
We realize that in times like these, it takes a God. Jesus, please
keep us near the cross; we don't want our living to be in vain.
Lord, teach us to be givers; we realize You
gave Your son, and Your son gave His life,
that whosoever believe in Him,
should not perish, but have
everlasting life. Lord, please teach
us to live according to the word
of God, so someday we can
go home to live with
You forever.

Amen.

61

Press On

Brethren, I count not myself to have apprehended: but this one thing I do, forgetting those things which are behind, and reaching forth unto thine things which are before, I press toward the mark for the prize of the high calling of God in Christ Jesus. Philippians 3:13-14

———————————

Almighty God, there are times
that we feel that all is lost, and there
is nowhere to turn. And we weep, weep and
weep, as if there is no hope.
But, then a still small voice from within
speaks to our spirit and encourages
us to press on in the name of the Lord.

It reminds us that Jesus paid it all
and all to Him we owe. Sin has left
a crimson stain, but His blood has
washed us white as snow.

Lord, please bring us closer to Your
heart and nurture us with Your praise.
Help us to realize You can still use our
broken lives, and Your infinite power to
put the pieces back together again.

Lord, help us to realize we are
frail creatures of the moment.
But, help us to know there is a
Light at the end of the tunnel where
everyone must go, and meet our Master.
And, if we have lived according to
the Bible, He will say, "Well done
thou good and faithful servant;
thou has been faithful over
a few things, and now I will
make you ruler over many.
Enter now into the joys of life".

Amen! Amen! Amen!

A Prayer of Gratefulness

I will bless the Lord at all times: His Praise shall continually
be in my mouth. My soul shall make its boast in the Lord;
The humble shall hear of it and be glad. O, magnify the Lord
with me, and let us exalt His name together. Psalm 34:1-3

Oh, Lord God of heaven,
Oh, Great and awesome God,
You who keep Your covenant and
mercy with those who love You
and observe Your commandments.

Thank You for knowing us, and loving us,
just as we are. Thank You for being a
loving Father who watches over us in
all of the places we go. Search our
hearts, try our thoughts; where
there is weakness in us, we pray
that You remove it, so that Your
name may be glorified.

Thank You for our families,
our friends, and our loved ones.
Thank You for our brothers and sisters
in the Body of Christ.
Thank You for using the callings, gifts, talents,
and abilities within the *Body of Christ* to edify
and equip the saints for the work of the ministry,
till we all come to the unity of the faith and of
the knowledge of the Son of God.
May we, too, apply our hearts to wisdom
and walk in such a way that we will redeem
the times that are ours. Grant us Your
presence that we may bring glory to
Your name by how we live for,
and how we serve You.

We thank You for the precious promise
that You will never leave nor forsake us.
Thank You for protecting and keeping us
even when we were not aware.

Grant that our faith and confidence
in You will never fade.
In Jesus' name we pray.

Amen.

Pastor, Henry T. Busby, Sr.
Mount Olive Baptist Church
Sapulpa, Oklahoma

A Servant Of the Lord

And He stretched forth His hand toward His disciples
and said, behold My mother and My brethren! For whosoever shall
do the will of My Father which is in heaven, the same is My Brother
and Sister and Mother. Matthew 12:49-50

————————

O Lord, our living bread that came down from heaven
to give life to the world! Lord, we thank You so much for
having sent to us Your servant, Your missionary who has
taught us the truth and made us sharers in Your grace.

We thank You Lord, for loving Mothers, who are always
lending a helping hand and always willing to share. Lord,
we realize that Mothers are special gifts from You and they
serve faithfully and give guidance wherever they are called
to strengthen our love for the church, the community and
others in need of prayer.

Mothers are someone who really cares.
I am Thankful to You God
for blessing me to have a Mother.
And most of all, I cherish having You
as my Savior and, Lord, we ask that You continue to
bless Your servants in good times, bad times,
happy times, and sad times. These are the blessings
we ask in Your name.

Amen.

Elder Kenny Blackwell
Tulsa, Oklahoma

His Spirit of Love

"Though the mountains be shaken and the hills be removed, yet My unfailing love for you will not be shaken nor My covenant of peace be removed, "says the Lord, who has compassion on you. Isaiah 54:10

O Holy Spirit, Dove Divine
Enter now Thy special place
with splendor, the heart within.

Spirit of Love,
Take me within Thy realm of peace.
Let Thy peace pervade my every step.
Step by step every day, every night,
Always and forever, never let go
Thy precious grasp.

Sweet, Sweet Spirit,
stay and spread Thy love to every heart
and home. We can only truly live within
Thy Sweet Embrace. Joy is everywhere Thou
hovers and dwells. Up to the sky and down to
earth, everywhere and all around, life blooms and blossoms
with Thee. Take hold of this moment
of True Beauty and Joy and make it
forever ours and us Yours.

Amen.

Dr. Mozella Mitchell
Chair, Department Religious Studies
University of South Florida
Tampa, Florida

Renewing our Love with God

Create in me a clean heart. O God; and renew a right spirit
within me. Cast me not away from Thy presence and take
not Thy holy spirit from me. Psalm 51:10-11

Lord . . . before we pray for land, we pray that
You will equip us for repentance.
Lord, renew the spirit in our lives.
Renew the love in our lives,
remove pollution and everything
that is not like You.

Lord, anoint our eyes that we may see
what You want us to be.
Let us be a living church and not a dead one.
Let the vitality of Your love refresh us,
that we move in power.
We pray that You would move in our land.
Bless our government to be a government
that follows the living God and others
will see the need to serve the Lord
as never before.

Amen.

VI
Prayers:
Work and Prosperity

*Be ye strong; therefore, and let not
your hands be weak: for your work shall
be rewarded. 2 Chronicles 15:7*

A Prayer for those In the Workplace

And whatsoever ye do, do it heartily, as to the Lord, and not unto men; knowing that of the Lord ye shall receive the reward of the inheritance; for ye serve the Lord Christ. Colossians 3: 23-24

Lord my God, Look down on us.
Life has changed so much in our workplace;
on the job most of our colleagues and
co-workers have gone. They are out of work.
Suddenly, what seemed so secure is now so
very fragile. It's hard to know what we feel:
sadness, uncertainty and fear of the future.
But Lord, we thank You for still having a job
to go to. But the question is? Who will be
next to be relieved of their job?

Who will be the next to be put on part—time
work? Who will be next? Lord, please help us
to cope with the increased duties and the
pressures of work.

Lord Jesus, in the midst of this uncertainty,
please; give us the strength to keep going and to
work to the best of our ability, taking each day
one at a time, and taking time each day to walk
with You. Help us to always remember that You
are the way, the truth and the life.

Amen.

A Prayer for Financial Stability

For ye remember, brethren, our labour and travail: for labouring night
and day, because we would not be chargeable unto any of you,
we preached unto you the gospel of God. 1Thessalonians 2:9

O Lord God,
We are living in disturbing days:
Throughout and across the world people
are suffering due to our economic crisis.

Prices are rising,
Debt is increasing,
Banks are collapsing,

and many jobs are taken away from people
who are in dire need of work. Our fragile
security is under threat.

Loving God, remove our fear and hear our
prayer: Lord, we are asking You to be a tower of
strength amidst the shifting sands, and a light
in the darkness; bless us so that we may receive
Your gift of peace, and fix our hearts where true
joys are to be found in Jesus Christ our Lord.

Amen.

A Prayer: For Those in Debt

But my God shall supply all your needs according to
His riches in glory by Christ Jesus. Philippians 4:19

O most merciful Father,
The fountain of all wisdom,
we pray for the many who are trapped
by growing burdens of debt.
Some see no way out, and only see
despair for their future.

Please give them courage to tackle
the problems they face.
Help them to make the right decisions
which will turn their situation around,
and give them faith that,
as they Pray to You in their trouble,
You will help relieve them of their stress.
Lord we know, You are strong enough
and You never fail those who trust in You.
Lord, please, keep them
under Your protection and
help them through their
time of darkness; give wisdom to all
who seek Your help, and bring them to the true
knowledge of freedom in
Your Son, Jesus Christ our Lord.

Lord, You know our needs before we ask:
Have compassion
on our weakness, and give us those things
that we need; not necessarily what we want.

Lord, we thank You for what You have done
and what You are going to do.
These blessings we ask
in Your Son Jesus' name.

Amen.

A Prayer: Those in Authority

Trust in the Lord with all thine heart; and lean not unto thine own understanding. In all thy ways acknowledge Him, and He shall direct thy paths. Be not wise in thine own eyes: fear the Lord and depart from evil. Proverbs 3: 5-8

Almighty Father,
whose will is to restore all things
in Your beloved Son, the King of all.
Please, govern the hearts and minds of those
in authority and bring the families of the nations,
divided and torn apart by the ravages of sin,
to be subject to His just and gentle rule;
who is alive and reigns with You,
in the unity of the Holy Spirit,
one God, now and forever.
God, our refuge and strength,
bring near the day when wars shall
cease and poverty and pain shall end,
that earth may know the peace of
heaven through Jesus Christ our Lord.

Amen.

Moving Against Giants

Though I walk in the midst of trouble, Thou wilt revive me:
Thou shalt stretch forth Thine hand against the wrath of mine
enemies, and Thy right hand shall save me. Psalm 138:7

Father in the name of our Lord and
Savior Jesus Christ we pray for
people that are coming against
spiritual, physical and natural giants.

We know that You have dealt with many giants.
You stand over and above all giants; above all
power and authorities, above all failure and
weakness. We ask that You please release Your
spirit throughout the church. Move from aisle to
aisle, window to window, pew to pew and from
person to person.

We have seen You move before. Now, Lord do
it again and again. We love You for what You
have done and what You will do. We will praise
Your name. Forever and ever!

Thank You, Jesus!

Amen.

A Prayer of Forgiving

And when ye stand praying, forgive, if ye have sought against any:
that your Father also which is in heaven may forgive you your
trespasses. But if ye do not forgive, neither will your Father
which is in heaven forgive your trespasses. Mark 11:25-26

Lord, if we have wounded any soul today, if we
have caused one foot to go astray, if we have walked
in our on willful way, Dear Lord forgive.

Dear Lord forgive our thoughts, deeds,
Misunderstanding of myself and others,
Our secret sin we have confessed to Thee.
Lord, even in our moments of being alone,
You have always been there just when
we needed You most.
Lord, please, teach us Thy ways and help us
to understand and walk in them.
For our darkness, You have been our light,
For our weakness, You have been our strength.,
For our loneliness, You have been our comforter.
My God, when we lay down to sleep, we pray to
The Lord our soul to keep, and if we should die
Before we awake, we pray to the Lord our soul
to take.
Amen.

VII
Prayers of Comfort

*Thank You, Jesus, that Your Spirit brings such comfort to my heart.
When I am sad or frighten, remind me that all I need to do is
open myself to You.*

Prayer: God Comforts

As one whom his mother comfortheth, so will I comfort you;
and ye shall be comforted in Jerusalem. Isaiah 66:13

Spirit of the living God,
fall fresh on me;
Break me, melt me,
mold me, fill me.
Spirit of the living God,
fall fresh on me.

O Lord our God,
Thank You, for Your spirit
that brings so much comfort to our
lives. When we are sad, help us to know
that all we need to do is to open
ourselves up and Your love will wrap
around us like a warm comforting blanket
and comfort us.
Thank You Lord for being a
Blanket to our souls.

Amen.

A Prayer Of Faith

"But without faith, it is impossible to please Him: for he that
cometh to God must believe that He is and that He is a
Rewarder of them that diligently seek Him. Hebrews 11:6.

God of all Creation,
Show us Your presence. Let us feel
Your love. Give us the courage and
generosity to respond to Your call.
Give us hearts that love and seek Your love;
Give us eyes that see the goodness in everyone.
In the good things that come our way today.

God, we give You praise.
In the things that are not so good,
please deepen our faith so that we may
realize that You are forever within us.
You have blessed us with many gifts, God;
we know it is our task to realize them.
May we never underestimate our potential;
may we never lose hope. May we find the strength
to strive for better, the courage to be different,
and the energy to give all that we have to offer
As we walk by faith in Jesus' name.

Amen.

Reverend Scott Gordon
Calvary Baptist Church
Sapulpa, Oklahoma

Sometimes We Have to Cry

In my distress I called upon the Lord, and cried to my God:
and He did hear my voice out of His temple, and my
cry did enter into His ears. II Samuel 22:7

If when you give the best of your service,
telling the world, that the Savior has come,
be not dismayed when men don't believe you.
He will understand and say, "Well done."

Sometimes in this life, we have to cry,
Nothing is hurting, but we cry,
Nobody has said anything about us,
but we cry, Not weary, but we cry,
Not depressed, but we cry.

Lord, many times in our life's experiences,
we have to cry. We really do not have any
specific reason why we cry,
but the Lord said, "He hears our cry".
He will allow us to see through
the eyes of faith a perfect day with
no clouds in the sky, no rain,
just a perfect day.

And in that day, the Lord Himself,
will come all the way down from heaven,
just to wipe our weeping eyes, and
we all will understand it better, by and by.

Amen.

Prayers For Those Who Mourn

And I will pray the Father, and He shall give you another
Comforter, that He may abide with you forever. John 14:16

———————

O Lord our God, we pray for Thy comforting spirit
to abide this day upon all who mourn;
Lord, we thank You for Your Holy Spirit.
Lord, You know our hearts and share our sorrows.
Lord, You know our hurt because of the loss
of the one we love.
Lord, we long for words of comfort,
Yet we find them hard to hear.
Lord please, turn our grief to truer living,
our affliction to firmer hope
in Jesus' name we pray.
Amen.

———————

O Gracious God,
surround us, and all who mourn this
day with Your continuing compassion.
Do not let grief overwhelm Your children,
or turn them against You. When grief
seems never-ending, take them one step
at a time along your road of death and
resurrection in Jesus Christ our Lord.

Amen.

Prayer: A Family Who Lost A Loved-One

Fear thou not; for I am with thee: be not dismayed;
for I am Thy God: I will strengthen thee; yea, I will help thee; yea,
I will uphold thee with the right hand of My righteousness. Isaiah 41:10

Eternal God, our Heavenly Father.
The giver of life and every important gift.
You are great and Your name is unaltered
above all that is in the earth. We come to
You on behalf of this family because of the
passing of a loved-one. You are the director
of all the affairs of men; You make no
mistakes; whatever You do is right.

Because of our humanity, we ask for this
family in their time of bereavement the faith
and strength to endure the departure of this
their loved-one from this earthly life. May they
serenely face the days to come with a deepened
trust in Thee. Give them the power to live in
greater faithfulness to the life of the unseen
world where the souls of the righteous are in
peace and the eternal ties of those we have lost
are never broken.

Lord, help this family to proclaim Your precious
promise: "Weeping may endure for the night
but joy comes in the morning. "Grant that they
may be brought through this experience to offer
themselves of renewed dedication in Your service,
ever submitting themselves in patience to Your
Divine will.

Help every one of us, O God, to consider the
uncertainty of life, that we may live in readiness
for Thy call to us, and when we have wound up
the last ball of trouble and jumped the last ditch
of sorrow, take us to that fair and distant land
where the wicked shall cease from troubling and
the weary shall be at rest, where all of God's sons
and daughters can sit at His feet and be blessed.
We ask these blessings in the name of Jesus
Christ, our Savior and Lord.

Amen.

Dr. G. Calvin McCutchen, Sr.
Pastor Emeritus
Mt. Zion Baptist Church
Tulsa, Oklahoma
Author: "One Of The Whosoevers"

Giving The Best of Your Service

His Lord said unto him, well done, thou good and faithful servant: thou hast been faithful over a few things, I will make thee ruler over many things: enter thou into the joy of Thy Lord. Matthew 25:21

If when you give the best of your service,
telling the world that the Savior has come.
He will understand and say "Well done".
We thank God that only He knows the
inner personality. He understands the silent
sigh of the beat of the heart, the longing of
the heart, and the cry of every heart.

And not only does He know,
He cares when we are hurt or
beaten down from life's problems,
He understands the longing of the soul.
And He knows how to mend a broken
heart. Thank You Lord, for loving us
enough to put salve on our wounds,
and attend our bleeding soul.

Amen.

Brokenness
Healer of A Broken Heart

The Lord is nigh unto them that are of a broken heart;
and saveth such as be of a contrite spirit. Many are the
afflictions of the righteous but the Lord delivereth
him out of them all. Psalm 34: 18-19

O God, send Your anointing in this place,
Let the word become flesh and dwell
among us. Somebody needs to know
that You are a problem solver,
You are a way maker,
You are a door opener, and a
lifter-up of a bowed-down head.

Lord, they need to know, that You care
for the brokenness in our lives. And in many
cases, we have made a mess of our lives.
But You know how to deal with a broken heart
and a contrite spirit. Let Your anointing heal
the brokenness in our hearts, and speak to our
broken spirits. Restore the joy we once felt
in Your love and patience.
Thank You, Lord.

Amen.

He Will Understand

And the peace of God, which passeth all understanding,
shall keep your hearts and minds through Christ Jesus. Philippians 4:7

God understands; He knows all about us.
He'll understand our broken promises;
He'll understand the pain and heart ache
you have encountered.

He'll understand the loneliness, and your
trials and tribulations, the time you will
stand alone, the desires of your heart.
He'll understand when family and friends
walk away.

He' s God and He knows who we are,
He understand your successes and failures,
our day-to-day disappointments, the
imperfections of our life.

He will understand the rock in the road;
He will understand our stumbling blocks
and make them stepping-stones. We thank
You God for Your peace, which passeth all
understanding and shall keep our hearts
and minds through Jesus Christ.

He will understand and say,
"Well Done . . ."

Amen.

God's Salvation

Whom having not seen, ye love: in whom, though now ye see Him not, yet believing, ye rejoice with joy unspeakable and full glory: receiving the end of your faith, even the salvation of your souls. 1 Peter 1:8-9

And in that day Thou shall say, "O Lord, I will praise Thee:
though Thou was angry with me, Thine anger is turned
away, and Thou comforted me
Behold, God is my salvation;
I will trust, and not be afraid;
For the Lord Jehovah is my strength
and my song: He also is my salvation.
Therefore, with joy shall we draw water
out of the wells of salvation.

And in that day shall ye say, "Praise the Lord,
Call upon His name, declare His doings among
the people, make mention that His name is exalted." Sing
unto the Lord; for He has done excellent things;This is
known in all the earth. Cry out and shout Thou inhabitant of
Zion: For great is the Holy One of
Israel in the midst of Thee.

Amen.

God Grant Us Serenity

The peace of God is beyond all human understanding.
His peace will guard your hearts and minds as you
live in Christ Jesus. Philippians 4:7.

God, give us grace to accept with serenity
The things that cannot be changed,
and the Wisdom to distinguish the one
from the other. Living one day at a time,
Enjoying one moment at a time, Accepting
hardship as a pathway to peace, Taking,
as Jesus did, This sinful world as it is, Not
as we would have it, trusting that You will
make all things right, If we surrender to
Your will, so that We may be reasonably
happy in this life, And supremely happy
with You forever.

Amen.

Inspired by:
_____Reinhold Niebuhr

VIII
Prayers
Ministers and the Church

God, may we keep growing closer and closer to You,
more and more like Your Son. Amen.

Church Family Prayer
Praying For Others

Wherefore comfort yourselves together, and edify
one another, even as also ye do. Thessalonians 5:11

———————

Mighty and eternal God,
You promised if two or three would gather
in Your name, You would be in the midst.
Lord, we want to thank You.

Thank You, through dangers seen
and unseen. You led us, and fed us,
guided and provided for us,
across the highways and the skyways.
And, we thank You.

Lord, we come from different walks of life,
but You know all about us. We are here
due to different circumstances and You know
the homes from which we have come.
You know, the places of our pain; You know
the places where we are weak, You know
where we fail; You know how we feel on the
inside. You know where sickness is raging
and tearing up homes and breaking hearts.
You know where drugs, alcohol, and substance
abuse are ripping at the fabric of Hope.

You know where the communication has shut
down between parent and child. You know
all about us, and we bring
You the broken pieces
of our dreams and lives.
We bring them to You because
You are able to take the broken pieces
and make a brand new person.

So, here we are, Lord,
confessing our needs in our personal
lives. We need You, in our family's lives;
We need You in our children's lives;
We need You in our daily lives.
We need You every hour.
We just need You, Lord.

Amen.

A Prayer For Preachers

Fear Thou not; for I am with thee: be not dismayed: for I am thy God.
I will strengthen thee; yea, I will help thee. Yea, I will uphold thee
with the right hand of My righteousness. Isaiah 41:10

————————

Our gracious Father in Heaven,
we accept with grateful hearts
this most wonderful privilege
of entering into Thy presence
through prayer.

We have prayed for help and
health for others, but now we
come to Thee for ourselves.
How greatly do we need a
strength that is more than human?
We find ourselves insufficient for
the task of today and each day.
Our vision is so narrow, our
judgment so faulty, our wishes
so incomplete. And now we put
out all before Thee; our cares that
Thou mayest care for us.
Our fear that Thou mayest still Them;
Our hope and wishes that they may be
granted not according to our will, but
according to Thou good will;
Our sins that Thou mayest forgive them,
Our thoughts and our desires that
Thou mayest cleanse them, and
Our whole life that Thou mayest
use it to Thine own honor and glory.
Life is sometimes hard and our faith is
easily shaken. Too often we have
compromised and left things half done.

Help us to see ourselves as Thou sees
us. Save us from contentment with small gains.
Deliver us from failure in endeavors; from being
too easily discouraged; from giving up and giving
in too soon, and from allowing any task to defeat
us because it is too difficult.

Grant that our feebleness may be turned
into strength, our failures point toward
success, and our fears be changed to
courage. We know we are weak
but we pray to be saved from failure.

Help us to remember that we have
the vows of God upon us. Our hands
have gripped the gospel plow, and we
have gone too far to turn back.
Endure us with the spirit
to forgive even when it is human
to seek revenge.
Kindle within us the desire to
do right and undergird our
weakness with Thy divine strength
that it may be done. Make us
faithful shepherds of Thy flock,
true seers of God, and true
followers of Jesus Christ,
for it is in His name we pray.

Amen.

Dr. G. Calvin McCutchen, Sr.
Pastor Emeritus
Mt. Zion Baptist Church
Tulsa, Oklahoma

A Prayer For The Church and Ministry

And He is the head of the body, the church. He is
The Beginning, the Firstborn from the dead, that in everything
He might be preeminent. Colossians 1:18

Dear Father God:
We come into Your presence thanking You
for our church. We praise You for Your goodness
and Your mercy. We recognize that You are God
and besides Thee there is no other.
We thank You that we all speak
the same thing.

There is no division among us;
We are perfectly joined together
in the same mind and the same spirit.
We confess that none of our members will
be children tossed to and fro and carried
about with every wind of doctrine.
We speak the truth in love.
We are a growing and maturing body
of believers who are strong in our
faith and belief in You, Lord.
Father, we thank You that every need
for this ministry has been met. Our church
is prospering financially, and we have more
than enough to meet every situation.
We have everything we need to carry out the vision of this
church . . . because of You.

Father, we also thank You
for the out-pouring of Your Holy Spirit
and the gifts that You placed in our church
and that You allow these gifts to flow
freely in the church.

We bind the spirit of failure off this ministry,
and we loose a spirit of success in Jesus' name. Father, we
count it all done and we praise You for it.
In Jesus' name we pray.

Amen.

Mrs. Edna Tisdale Marz
Mt. Zion Free Will Baptist Church
Fayetteville, North Carolina

A Call To God

Lord, Thou hast been our dwelling place in all generations.
Before the mountains were brought forth, or even
Thou hadst formed the earth
and the world, even from everlasting to everlasting,
Thou art God. Psalm 90

Almighty and most merciful God,
We come just to say thank You for all of Your
many blessings. We thank You for protecting
us last night as we slept like dead men and
women. We thank You that the family circle
was not broken, and You allowed us another
chance to make our way to Your house of
prayer one more time.

Since we met last, many are sick and some
have gone, to try a world unknown to man.
But thank God, we are here standing on Your
promise and we cannot do anything until
You come.

There are those with broken hearts and broken
promises. There are those that are confused and
don't know which way to go; there are those that
need to make a decision, and there are those that
are lost and need help.
Lord, please come into our lives, move in our
lives, and let us continue to feel Your presence.
These and all blessings we ask in Your name.

Amen.

Spiritual Leaders

And Ruth said, Intreat me not to leave Thee, or to return
from following after thee: for whither thou goest I will go;
and where thou lodgest I will lodge: thy people shall be
my people, and thy God my God. Ruth 1:16

O God, Almighty Father:
We thank You for our Spiritual Leaders,
We thank you for all they do.
God please continue to keep them and
richly bless them throughout their lives.

Lord, we thank You for blessing them
to be the thread that keeps us
together years without end,
and showing and teaching us how
to forgive and always remain friends.

Lord, You have blessed them to always
show love to everyone they meet.
Lord, Your love shines through them
in all they say and do.
Lord, they are gifts from heaven,
always working to help those less
fortunate, those without homes, clothing,
and without food on their table.
Lord, please bless our spiritual leaders
now and always until we meet
on the other side and be forever friends.

Amen.

Reverend William Holloway
Oklahoma City, Oklahoma

Jesus: Jesus Is the Name

Be it known unto you all, and to all the people of Israel, that by
the name of Jesus Christ of Nazareth, whom ye crucified,
whom God raised from the dead, even by Him doth this
Man stand here before you whole Acts: 4:10

Jesus, Jesus, Jesus
There is something about that name.
Kings and kingdoms will all fade away but
there is something about that name
that is everlasting!
O how we love the name Jesus.
Lord, we can't praise You enough.
Lord we know there is healing in Your
name; there is also peace, consolation,
Joy and happiness in Your name.
Lord, we kneel in Your presence and
give You the praise forever and forever.

Glory!

God Is God All By Himself

For there is one God, and one mediator between God and men,
the man Christ Jesus; Who gave Himself a ransom for all,
to be testified in due time. 1 Timothy 2:5-6.

———————

Omnipotent King, Lion of Judah,
Rock of Ages, Prince of Peace,
King of Kings, Lord of Lords,
Provider, Protector, Paternal Leader
Ruling Lord, and Reigning King
of the entire universe. He is our
Father, He is our Helper,
He is our Guardian, and He is God.

He is the First and Last,
the Beginning and the End.
He is the keeper of Creation
and the Creator of all. He is
the Architect of the universe
and the Manager of all times.

He always was, He always is,
and He always will be Unmoved,
Unchanged, Undefeated, and
never Undone. He was pierced
in the side. He was persecuted
and bought freedom.
He was dead and brought to life.
He is risen and brings power.
He reigns and brings Peace.
The world can't understand Him,
the armies can't defeat Him;

the schools can't explain Him,
and the leaders can't ignore Him.
Herod couldn't kill Him;
the Pharisees couldn't confuse Him,
and the people couldn't hold Him!
Nero couldn't crush Him;
Hitler couldn't silence Him;
the New Age can't replace Him;
He is light, love, longevity, and Lord.

He is Goodness, Kindness,
Gentleness, and God. He is Righteous,
Mighty, Powerful, and Pure. His ways
are right. His world is eternal; His will is
unchanging. He is our redeemer;
He is our Savior; He is our guide, and
He is our peace. He is our Joy; He is
our comfort; He is our Lord and
He rules our lives.

We serve Him because His bond is love;
His burden is light. We follow Him
because He is the wisdom of the wise,
the power of the powerful, the ancient
of days, the ruler of rulers the leader of
leaders, the overseer of the over comers,
and the sovereign Lord of all that was and is to
come. His goal is a relationship with you. He
will never leave you, never forsake you, never
mislead you, never forget you, never overlook
you. When you call him He will lift you up.
When you fail, He forgives.
When you are weak, He will strengthen
You; when you are lost, He is the way
when you are afraid. He will be your courage.

105

When you are hungry, He will feed you.
When you face problems, He will comfort you.
He is everything for everybody, everywhere,
every time, and every way. He is faithful.
He is in control.

For God . . .
Is God All by Himself!

Unknown

Amen

A Prayer:
Church Leadership

And whosoever of you will be the chiefest, shall be servant of all. For even the Son of Man came not to be ministered unto, but to minister, and to give His life a ransom for many. Mark 10:44-45

O God Our Father.
Please come into
our church with the
spirit of revival. Lord,
continue to bless
our church leaders
with Your Power, so
we may constantly see
the message of the
gospel flow within
them, through them
and in their lives.
In Jesus' Name

Amen.

107

IX
Prayers
For
Peace and Humanity

The Lord lift up His countenance upon thee,
and give thee peace. Numbers 6:26.

A Prayer For Peace

And the peace of God, which passeth all understanding,
shall keep your hearts and minds through Christ Jesus. Philippians 4:7

Peace I leave with you, My peace I give to you: not as the
world giveth, give I unto you. Let not your heart be troubled,
neither let it be afraid. John 14:27

Lord God of compassion,
whose will is for peace built on
righteousness; we pray for peace, peace in
the home, in the family, and peace in the
community. Lord, we pray for an end to
hostilities and for comfort, and we pray for help
for all who suffer. We pray for reconciliation
between the countries of Palestine and Israel,
Iran and Iraq, and peace throughout the
world, through Jesus Christ,
the Prince of Peace.

Amen.

*For Thou hast been a
strength to the poor,
a strength to the
needy in his distress,
a refuge from the storm,
a shadow from the heat,
when the blast of the
terrible ones is as a storm
against the wall. Isaiah 25:4*

Amen.

Prayer: People In Developing Countries

Open thy mouth for the dumb in the cause of all such as
are appointed to destruction. Open thy mouth, judge righteously,
and plead the cause of the poor and needy. Proverbs 31: 8-9

O Lord, My God,
Please look down on the suffering
People throughout the world, especially in
developing countries. Many are forced to
live amid deterioration, disease and despair.
We raise our voices on their behalf, as
truth-tellers we want to
proclaim "This is not good."
It is not how You desire our
world to be. Loving Father, look
after the millions of people who are
homeless, millions of people who are
hungry. Please Father, care for the little
ones, comfort the dying ones, and into their
hour of darkness may Your light begin to shine.
Thank You, Lord.

Amen.

A Prayer for the People of Haiti

For He hath not despised nor abhorred the affliction of the afflicted; neither hath He hid His face from him; but when he cried unto Him, He heard. Psalm 22: 24

God, Loving parent of all,
Please look down on the people of Haiti
and Bless them. Help them to know
that they are not a forgotten people,
that You will comfort them, their families,
women and children.
Lord, they are homeless, displaced,
wounded, and orphaned due to disasters
and conflicts in Caribbean Countries and Africa.
Lord, please give the people within these
countries and the continent hope and
courage to seek enduring peace
with justice and freedom,
that their children might grow up without fear;
for the sake of your Son,
Jesus Christ.

Amen.

Know ye that the LORD He is God:
it is He that hath made us,
and not we ourselves; we are His people,
and the sheep of His pasture.
Enter into His gates with thanksgiving,
and into His courts with praise:
be thankful unto Him, and bless His name.
For the LORD is good;
His mercy is everlasting; and His truth endureth
to all generations. Psalm 100:3-5

A Mission
of Love and Compassion

Behold I stand at the door, and knock: If any man hear My voice,
and open the door, I will come in to him and will sup with him
and he with Me. Revelations 3:20

O Lord my God,
Please remember our friends.
Lord, they have prayed for us, and
they have taken care of us.

Lord, You have given us the desire
to join with one another in our
common prayer. We remember Your promise
that when two or three are gathered together in
Your name, You will grant our requests,
our prayers, and fulfill our desires. Lord, grant us,
above all else, a knowledge of Your truth in
this world and everlasting life with You.
These are the blessings we ask in Your name.

Amen.

Dr. Francine Thomas
Anchorage, Alaska

2

A Prayer for Refugees

By faith he sojourned in the land of promise, as in a strange country, dwelling in tabernacles with Isaac and Jacob, the heirs with him of the same promise: For he looked for a city which hath foundations, whose builder and maker is God.
Hebrews 11:9-10

Almighty and merciful God,
whose Son became a refugee
and had no place to call His own;
please, look with mercy on those
who today are fleeing from danger,
who are homeless and hungry.
Bless those who work to bring them
relief; inspire generosity and
compassion in all our hearts; and
guide the nations of the world
towards that day when all will
rejoice in Your Kingdom of justice
and of peace; through Jesus Christ
our Lord.

Amen.

Prayers for Mercy

For He saith to Moses, I will have mercy on whom I will have mercy,
and I will have compassion on whom I will have compassion.
So then it is not of him that willeth, nor of him that runneth,
but of God that sheweth mercy. Romans 9:15-16.

O God of Mercy,
remember Christ Your Son
who is peace Himself and who has
washed away our hatred with His blood.
Because You love all people,
look with mercy on us. Banish
the violence and evil within us,
and in answer to our prayers,
restore tranquility and peace.

Amen.

Grant us Lord God,
A vision of our land as Your love would make it
A land where the weak are protected,
and none are poor or go hungry;
A land where the benefits of civilized life are
Shared and everyone can enjoy them;
A land where different races and cultures
live in tolerance and mutual respect;
A land where peace is built with justice,
and justice is guided by love.
And please, give us the inspiration and courage
to build it, through Jesus Christ our Lord.

Amen.

A Prayer:
Leaders of Nations

O Praise the Lord, all ye nations: praise Him, all ye people.
For His merciful kindness is great toward us: and the truth of the
Lord endureth forever. Praise ye the Lord. Psalm 117.

O God our heavenly Father,
whose love sets no boundaries
and whose strength is in service.
Grant to the leaders of the nations
Wisdom, courage and insight at this
time of darkness and fear.

Give to all who exercise authority
and determination to defend
the principles of freedom and love,
tolerance and strength to protect
and safeguard the innocent; and
clarity of vision to guide the world
into the paths of justice and peace.
This we ask through
Jesus Christ our Lord.

Amen.

A Prayer For
The Government

EXHORT therefore, that, first of all, supplications,
prayer, Intercessions, and giving of thanks,
be made for all men. 1 Timothy 2:1

Our Heavenly Father,
The source of all truth and wisdom,
who knows and loves the whole creation,
please watch over our nation:
So, that truth may prevail over distortion,
wisdom triumph over recklessness
and the concerns of every person be heard.

Lord Jesus, help us to support policies that sustain
the poor, the vulnerable, and the frightened people
of this world. Holy Spirit, who brought understanding
among myriad peoples and languages, please give a passion
for peace to all of Your people. Help there to be peace in the
world,
and inspire us to work for unity and co-operation
throughout the world and in our political life together.

Amen.

A Prayer For Protection

The one who offers thanksgiving as his sacrifice glorifies Me;
to one who orders his way rightly I will show
the salvation of God. Psalm 50:23

Almighty God,
thank You for Touching our bodies
this morning. And we were able to see
a brand new day. Through the night,
people were getting shot;
They were going to the hospital;
They were being put out, and
Many apartments and homes caught
fire; Children were sick with high
temperatures and fever.

There are those that lost everything.
But through it all, we can still say . . .
Thank You Lord,
Because You have been better
to us than we have been to ourselves.
Thank You for protecting and sheltering us
through the night, while ambulance and police cars
were protecting our streets. You protected us from
harm and danger and for that, we say "thank You, Lord."
Thank You for just keeping us clothed in our right mind, and
a mind to serve You.

Amen.

Ms. June Cobb
Oklahoma City, Oklahoma

X
Occasional Prayers

Pray at all times and on every occasion
in the power of the Holy Spirit. Stay alert
and be persistent in your prayers for all
Christians everywhere. And pray for Me, too.
Ephesians 6:18-19

Conforming to
The Lord's Prayer

And be not conformed to this world; but be ye transformed by
the renewing of your mind, that ye may prove what is that good,
and acceptable, and perfect, Will of God. Romans 12:2

We cannot say, OUR if our religion has no room for others
and their needs

We cannot say FATHER if we do not demonstrate this
relationship in our daily living.

We cannot say WHO ART IN HEAVEN if all our interests
and pursuits are in earthly things

We cannot say HALLOWED BE THY NAME if we, who are
called to bear His name, are not holy.

We cannot say THY KINGDOM COME if we are unwilling to
give up our own sovereignty and accept the righteous reign
of God.

We cannot say THY WILL BE DONE if we are unwilling or
resentful of having it in our lives.

We cannot say ON EARTH AS IT IS IN HEAVEN unless we
are truly ready to give ourselves to His service here and now.

We cannot say GIVE US THIS DAY OUR DAILY BREAD
without expending honest effort for it, or by ignoring the
genuine needs of others.

We cannot say forgive us OUR TRESPASSES AS WE FORGIVE those who trespass against us if we continue to harbor a grudge against anyone.

We cannot say LEAD US NOT INTO TEMPTATION if we deliberately choose to remain in a situation where we are likely to be tempted.

We cannot say DELIVER US FROM EVIL if we are not prepared to fight with the spiritual weapon of prayer.

We cannot say THINE IS THE KINGDOM if we do not give the King the disciplined obedience of a loyal subject.

We cannot say THINE IS THE POWER if we fear what our neighbors and friends may say or do.

We cannot say THINE IS THE GLORY if we are seeking our own glory first.

We cannot say FOREVER if we are too anxious about each day's events.

We cannot say AMEN unless we honestly say "Cost what it may, this is my prayer."

Amen.

Author Unknown

I Saw God Wash
The World Last Night

Wash me thoroughly from mine iniquity, and cleanse me from my sin.
Psalm 51:2 Purge me with hyssop and I shall be clean: wash me,
and I shall be whiter than snow. Psalm 51:7

——————

God washed the world last night
With His sweet showers on high;
And then when morning came
He hung it out to dry.

He washed each slender blade of grass
And every trembling tree;
He flung His showers against the hills
And swept the rolling sea.

The white rose is a deeper white;
The red, a richer red
Since God washed every fragrant face
And put them all to bed.

There's not a bird, there's not a bee
That wings along the way,
But is a cleaner bird and bee
Than it was yesterday.
We saw God wash the world last night;
Ah, would He had washed me
As clean of all my dust and dirt
As that old white birch tree!

Amen.

—William Stidger

Resurrection Prayers
(Easter Prayers)

I am He that liveth, and was dead; and, behold,
I am alive for evermore, Amen; and have the keys of hell
and death. Revelation 1:18

O Mighty and Heavenly Father,
pour upon us, Thou heavenly
blessing so that we may be armed
with the faith of the resurrection and
to fear no one.

Help us to truly understand
the meaning of Easter
and that our Father lives;
That He is alive,
That He is not the Great I Was,
But, He is the Great I AM.

He is not only a Fact, 'but "a living Fact".
He Lives, He lives within our souls.

Amen.

O heavenly Father,
whose blessed Son has risen from the
dead, grant that in His glory we may rise to
everlasting life. Lord, we also pray for all
our families and our neighbors, that we may
all share in a joyful resurrection and be
partakers of Thy heavenly kingdom,
through Christ our Lord.

Amen.

God our Father,
Let our celebration today
renew our lives by Your
Spirit that is within us.
Grant this through our Lord
Jesus Christ, your Son,
who lives and reigns
with You and the
Holy Spirit, one God,
Forever and ever.

Amen.

Lord of Creation and God of Grace,
we thank You for the yearly
miracle of the Resurrection.
Send into our hearts
Your Holy Spirit, to raise us
to newness of life and
to clothe us with the beauty
of Your Holiness, for Your honor and grace.

Amen.

A Prayer of Thanksgiving

Enter His gates with thanksgiving, and His counts with praise
give thanks to Him, bless His name. Psalm 100:4

———————

Our Father in Heaven,
In the name of Jesus we ask Your blessing
upon us during this Thanksgiving Season.
You have opened the windows of heaven
and given us blessings far beyond our capacity
to receive. We come to thank You today.
Bless our homes and our families. Give us
compassion for those who are not so blessed as we.

Bless today our great nation and President.
My we continue to strive to make it great.
Forgive the wrongs we often impose on
others and help us to live in peace and love for
our Fellow men. Bless our schools and our churches.
May we ever strive to make them as Thou would
have them to be. We thank Thee for freedom,
and give us determination to ever stand for the
Christian way of life. In the powerful, wonderful
and magnificent name of Jesus we pray.

Amen.

Pastor John A. Reed, Jr. and Dr. Pat Reed
Fairview Baptist Church
Oklahoma City, Oklahoma

A Christmas Prayer
A Prayer From the Heart

And the angel answered and said unto her, The Holy Ghost
shall come upon thee, and the power of the Highest shall
overshadow
thee: therefore also that holy thing which shall be born of thee shall
be called the Son of God. ~ Luke 1:35

Our Father in Heaven,
the Father of our Lord and Savior,
Jesus Christ. We thank Thee for the
Christmas Season.

It is a season of gladness
for most of us. Give our hearts concern for
those in need at this season.
May we plan to give as well as receive gifts.
As we think of the gift Jesus made for us,
may we be filled with concern for others.

Let there be in our hearts, as we again
Regard the Christ of the cradle,
new faith and hope for a better world.
Touch and make beautiful our lives this
season. It is our prayer, O God, that
You will bless all of our homes.
Give to each a lasting happiness
founded upon love for Christ.
Let the peace and happiness of
Christmas be ours today and each
day throughout the coming year.

May the meaning of Christmas be stronger
And brighter than ever before.
Bless our loved ones who are far away
and those close at hand.
Fill us with happy contentment and peace.
In the name of Christ we pray.

Amen.

Dr. John A. Reed, Jr.
Pastor, Fairview Baptist Church
Oklahoma City, Oklahoma

A New Years Prayer

Therefore, if any man be in Christ,
he is a new creature: old things are passed away;
behold, all things are become new. 2 Corinthians 5:17

Almighty and everlasting God:
Who makes all things new,
You are the Alpha and Omega,
the Beginning and the End, and
whose years shall not fail.

Another year has come and gone and
We thank you for allowing us to enter
the new year.

We ask you to please go with us as
we travel along the unknown paths
of this coming year and bring us closer
to Thee. With faithful hearts help us
to serve more faithfully, so that our lives may be a
testimony to Thee.

That in all things we may please Thee
and glorify Thy name.

Amen.

A Prayer
For the Coming Year

Remember ye not the former things, neither consider
the things of old. Behold, I will do a new thing; now it shall spring
forth; shall ye not know it? I will even make a way in the wilderness
and rivers in the desert. Isaiah 43: 18-19

O Father of Fathers
thank You for
remaining the same,
remaining a constant
from one year to the
next who are the same.

Grant us to pass through
the coming year with
faithful hearts, so that we
may be able to please You.
These are the blessing we
ask in Your name.

Amen.

An Opening Prayer
(Invocation)

Take heed therefore unto yourselves, and to all the flock, over which the Holy Ghost hath made you overseers, to feed the church of God, which He hath purchased with His own blood. Acts 20: 28.

Eternal God, Our Alpha and Omega,
The Beginning and the End,
we come at this time and in this
place to ask You to bless this
gathering. Lord enable us to do the work
that You would have us to do. Help us
to continue to serve our communities
locally, nationally and internationally,
and be a blessing to those who are less
fortunate. Lord, empower us to move
from darkness to light. May Your light
within us shine during our meetings,
our discussions, and our deliberations.

Lord, this is Your hour, we invite You
into this meeting; into this ceremony. Help
us to make the most of each precious moment.
We ask You to lead and guide us, so the
decisions we make would be pleasing to You

Amen.

A Closing Prayer

And He hath filled him with the Spirit of God, in wisdom,
in understanding and in knowledge, and in all manner
of workmanship. Exodus 35:31

———————

O Holy and merciful God
Our Gracious and loving Heavenly Father,
The Giver of every good and perfect gift,
bless Your servants that have assembled
here today.

Lord, as we prepare to leave this place
let Your Spirit of wisdom and understanding
be with us, give us the strength, and the
courage that we need to satisfy Your will. Give
us the perseverance that we need for the journey
that You have started us on, keep us safe in our
travel as we return to our homes. Let Your Spirit
of wisdom, and understanding be with us, and
remain with us, accompany us, to give us hope.
Lord please help us to always be mindful of the
need of others. We pray, in Jesus' name.

Amen.

Praying Hands

Humble yourselves therefore under the mighty hand
of God, that He may exalt you in due time. I Peter 5:6

———————

The *"Praying Hands"* are much,
much more
than just a work of art;
They are the "soul's creation"
of a deeply thankful heart
They are a *Priceless Masterpiece*
That love alone could paint,
And they reveal the selflessness
of an unheralded saint.
These hands so scarred and toil
worn, tell the story of a man
Who sacrificed his talent
in accordance with God's Plan-
For in God's Plan are many things
man cannot understand,
But we must trust God's judgment
And be guided by His Hand.
Sometimes He asks us to give up
Our dreams of happiness;
Sometimes we must forgo our hopes
Of fortune and success-
Not all of us can triumph or rise
to heights of fame,
And many times What *Should Be Ours,*
goes to *Another Name*

But he who makes a sacrifice,
so another may succeed,
Is indeed a true disciple
Of our blessed Savior's creed
For when we "give ourselves away"
In sacrifice and love,
We are "laying up riches treasures"
in God's Kingdom up above
And hidden in gnarled, toil worn hands
is the truest *Art of Living,*
Achieved alone by those who've learned
the *"Victory of Giving"*
For any sacrifice on earth,
made in the dear Lord's name,
Assures the giver of a place
in Heaven's Hall of Fame—
And who can say with certainty
Where the *Greatest Talent Lies,*
Or Who Will Be the Greatest
In Our Heavenly Father's Eyes!

—Helen Steiner Rice
Inspired by Albrecht Durer

About the Author

Reverend Erma J. Coburn, is a native of Oklahoma, a powerful, Holy Ghost-filled missionary who has traveled throughout the world spreading the good news of the Gospel of Jesus Christ. Some of her travels include several countries within the continent of Africa, Caribbean, Israel (Holy Land), Austria and Spain.

Reverend Coburn is a graduate of Booker T. Washington High School in Sapulpa, Oklahoma. While working in the church and during missionary work throughout the State of North Carolina, she received her ministerial license from Freewill Baptist Church in Fayetteville.

After the loss of her husband, Sgt. Albert V. Coburn, she relocated back to Oklahoma and continued her education earning the Bachelor's of Science in Theology at the Oklahoma School of Religion at Langston University.

She later returned to Langston, University, graduating with a Bachelor's Degree in Elementary Education. Her spiritual calling and revelation coupled with the gift and ability to teach, catapulted her into a traveling evangelism ministry. She pursued graduate studies at Oral Roberts University in Tulsa, Oklahoma and the University of South Florida in Tampa, Florida.

She taught in the Oklahoma City Public School System and retired after 25 years of service. Though retired, she is continuously sought to teach in the school system, churches, and serve on workshop panels for local, state and national religious conventions.

Reverend Coburn and Mrs. Donna Hall, her late sister, along with other Christian warriors established the Sapulpa City Wide Prayer Band in Sapulpa whose "Annual Day of Prayer" has been in existence for over 30 years.

Reverend Coburn is an instructor in the Oklahoma Baptist Convention and the East Zion District Association. She is an active member of the Fairview Baptist Church, where Reverend Dr. John A. Reed, Jr. is Pastor. She has two children, three grandchildren and four great-grand children. She resides in Oklahoma City, Oklahoma.